For Janet

Our Forever Ben

One Mom's letters
to her *son-in-spirit*
and his poetic replies

With love from

By Jamie Lee Silver
and Benjamin Lee Silver

*Jamie Lee Silver
& Ben!*

Special edition created in partnership with
Hope for the Day
www.hftd.org

When you lose a loved one, there's a need/desire/requirement to find a way to integrate your loved-one-in-spirit into your life in a new way. This work illustrates one mom's successful path to comfort through her unique form of journaling.

Journaling is a well respected technique used in grief work, it provides a written record of progress to savor and return to over and over again. It has the ability to inspire hope and motivation to move forward ~ embracing the idea that yes, you can live again.

Our Forever Ben takes journaling to the next level because it's interactive. When Jamie writes to Ben, and keeps her pen on the paper, she hears the voice of her son speaking, and writes the words she hears. In this way, the ongoing relationship is reciprocal. Ben's words become the building blocks for Jamie to embrace a present and a future WITH her son, not without him.

Through "Our Forever Ben," Jamie wishes to help others learn how easy and useful this technique can be. And through telling Ben's story she hopes that those who hear it will do whatever they can to positively influence the world of mental health. AND it is her fervent wish that if anyone who reads these words is considering taking their life that they stop, breathe, reach out for help and live.

In counseling terms, Jamie has found a way to demonstrate and teach the grief-work skill of building an adaptive narrative surrounding her son, including past, present and future. She can come to see what he meant in her life and what their relationship means right now, and have an ongoing real experience of what it will mean in the future. It's also notable that Jamie can write to Ben on her timetable, whenever she wants. The moment she needs comfort, she finds it, and so can you.

Jamie is a healthy individual, living a productive life and setting a positive example. She is dedicating her life to helping others, as she continues to write to Ben, and he continues to write her back.

Jamie's hope is that this book can serve as a source of comfort for others who have experienced the loss of a loved one. For additional thoughts and inspiration please visit Jamie's website at JamieLeeSilver.com.

Notes from Jamie

I'm Ben's Mom.
I will always be Ben's Mom.

And we'll always be together through the power of the written word.

Any time I want to communicate with Ben I write to him. After I write to him, while holding my pen on the paper, he writes back to me. Immediately. It always happens. It is as easy as breathing. And I'm writing this book to show you how easy it is to communicate with your loved one who has, as they say, "passed away," but I prefer to say "became eternal," or "loved-one-in-spirit."

I only speak what so many who love deeply already know.

Life is eternal; communication with those we've loved is natural. We don't have to be psychic. We just need to be open.

When we're open, words of love flow.

Before Ben "died," he didn't leave a note. I got my note a week later, in a moment of stillness at the pool in the sun. Through my own hand I got my note. And since that time he has written me over and over.

I decide to share our writings after becoming part of a suicide support group. I found that I was sad, of course, but because of my correspondence with Ben, I was not suffering from not getting a note. I was not wondering why he did it. And, above all, I felt the closeness that we always had together. I realized I could help people by sharing our story.

Because although Ben "lost" his battle, he also won. He won because we're writing this book together. He won because we launched the inaugural Ben's Memorial Mile on June 11th, 2016 to bring the community of runners, family members, friends together to honor Ben's life and raised $22,000 for a cure for schizophrenia. For more information about Ben's Memorial Mile go to BensMemorialMile.com

I dedicate this book to the millions of suicide loss survivors whose loved ones are now in spirit. May you gain strength, happiness and fulfillment by accessing this form of communication.

Here's the simple formula for you to try on your own. It requires a stretch of your imagination, and the willingness and desire to connect. It doesn't matter if you actually believe your loved one is writing to you. You can also think this is what he or she would say if they could. When you read it over, you will feel their love.

Step 1.

Write a letter to your loved one in spirit. Express your feelings, your sadness, anger love, whatever you feel. Use your favorite terms of endearment. Make this letter as long or short as you'd like.

Step 2.

Write an invocation. Ask them what they have to say to you.

Step 3

Keep your pen on the paper, listen and write. The first time I did this I had to scribble for a few moments, but soon, I heard my loved one speaking and just began to write. An open mind is all it takes. Don't judge the words. Don't think too much, just write.

If you have challenges with this, feel free to contact me for personal consulting at Jamie@JamieLeeSilver.com

This book is a special edition published in partnership with Hope For The Day(HFTD). HFTD is an amazing organization based in Chicago that focuses on suicide prevention and mental health education through self-expression platforms such as music and the arts. I am honored to partner with them on their signature campaign

called *It Only Takes One.* To learn more please visit
www.ItOnlyTakesOne.org.

We want to start with Ben's story...written through through his eyes. Please read this when you have a few moments to take it in, and have some tissues handy. It's a tough story. You can even skip it for now and go straight to the poetry section. Ben's story is not over because you're holding this book in your hands, it is not over. It will never be over. We have work to do.

Benjamin Lee Silver's story:

There was no place for me in this world. I was twenty-two years old and there was *no* place for me in this world. No place would take me. There was no halfway house for people like me. I was battling schizophrenia and the endless noise in my head.

I was stuck in this hospital. And then. Then they put a carnival with live music right across the street from the hospital...and I could see it and hear it...but I couldn't get out to go...

It wasn't always this way.

I had my share of good years. Even great years.

In my prime I could push my body to unbelievable feats of running success. I was celebrated by my teammates and my competitors, my family and my friends. Those were good years.

And when I wrote songs and poetry, and got to kiss a beautiful girl…those were excellent times.

My high school teammates and coaches called me a "beast." I was not tall, only 5'3", tough as nails in some ways, and prone to injury. My brain power amazed even me sometimes – one summer I earned 27 Advanced Placement credits on my own just by reading the books and taking the tests.. That's crazy, just crazy.

And every chance I got…I ran. High School and college coaches heard about my times. There was a buzz about Ben Silver, the Downers Grove runner.

One perfectly apple-crisp day in fall, when the leaves were golden and everything smelled ripe, I ran in my junior high cross country meet and Al Carius, the legendary North Central College coach came out to see me run. I was in 7th grade."

My older brother, a runner himself, put his arm around me, shook his head and said "It's the first of many Ben, the first of many. You're a running phenom."

All through Junior High, and High School, when I got injured I kept my heart rate up. I spent up to three hours a day on the elliptical machine, blasting music into my ears to dull the pain of the exercise. I knew I must be damaging my hearing, but I didn't stop. Maybe I knew I wouldn't need my hearing for too much longer. Maybe I "knew" I was using up my body, and wouldn't need it for long.

And in those days, in those brief and shining sun-lit days (or cold and wind-whipped days) I ran like the wind. I ran like the wind. I had fans I'd never met. I was recognized every year as a scholar, and an athlete. I always did my best to be a good guy, to welcome the younger runners to the family and to make people smile. I was captain of the team.

It wasn't always this way. I'd been called "stupid little shrimp" since third grade, and I took to standing up for those who were bullied or shunned. I liked going out of the way to make people laugh and smile. It came easily to me. My Mom always said I had perfect comic timing.

I graduated High School with a great athletic record. I was the first athlete from Downers Grove North High School to go to Cross Country State three times. What a run that was!

I pushed my body way beyond what it wanted. After each race I had to be practically carried to our team tent and my buddies would untie my shoes, because I just didn't have the strength.

This was all before everything went wrong and I could get nothing to go right.

See, I always wanted a full college scholarship for running. I just DID. I didn't need one. My grandmother was paying for college for me and all my cousins. But I wanted to earn a full scholarship – room and board. I had to prove that all those years of pain were worth something.

I had a phenomenal senior year. I found out I got the full scholarship to Miami of Ohio, and I continued to run well. For the year-end State Track Meet I was injured again, and only qualified for the slow two-mile heat. That meant I had to outrun my fellow racers in the slow heat by a huge distance because I was running for time, not against the other runners in the race.

There were what seemed like hundreds of families from Downers Grove on their feet screaming for me as I ran, all alone on the track, so far ahead of anyone else. I wouldn't find out if I medaled until after the next race, the fast heat, was run. My time had to beat their times. It had to be 9th fastest or better. And when I walked to the podium to stand with my peers and receive my medal, the top runners I'd raced against for six years said "You belong here Ben."

It was my last victory. But I didn't know it at the time.

That fall I entered Miami of Ohio with my full scholarship and an injured ankle that would not heal. Ever.

So here I was, at this school full of people so different from me, with a full running scholarship, no ability to prove myself through running and (I'm not kidding you), I was the shortest boy on campus.

I tried to fit in. I really did. I was required to go to all the practices, work outs, and meets, but I was never really part of the team. The coach took me to various doctors. One doctor took a look at my bowed legs, and right in front of me said to the coach "You paid for THAT?"

You paid for that?

And I never got my bearings. They didn't even have a student center where I could perform my original songs.

Most of the students knew what they wanted to do. Me? I didn't have a clue. I bounced around from one major to another. I started hearing a voice in my head declaring "There is no place for you in this world. You're a loser. You can't figure out what you want to be. And you can't run anymore. There is no place for you in this world."

So, I started leaving it.

I began researching hallucinogens. I became obsessed with them. I studied all about them on the web. Some said they gave you access to another world, a better world, only accessible from within. I was failing on the surface of my life. I had no real friends; I was short; useless, undirected…so I began ordering drugs from the internet and smoking pot. It brought me up. For the moment. But I always went back down.

Once, in the fall of sophomore year, I did try to run in a meet, even though my ankle was still injured. I failed miserably and barely finished the race. Again, there was no place for me in this world.

Second semester sophomore year Mom came to visit, but it was already too late. Too late. I was losing my grip. Something was going wrong in my mind.

Mom was worried about me. She didn't want me experimenting with drugs, but I'll tell you one thing, I always knew my own mind. It was hard to get me to do anything I didn't want to do – or to *not* do anything I'd set my mind on. I was always determined. That's how I'd become a running champion.

What I remember most about Mom's visit were my tears. My regret. I told her everything I'd ever done was a failure, everything I'd accomplished was a lie, every good thing was actually bad. I had started wondering if I was the same person anymore. Who was I in the past? Who am I now?

Mom tried to get me to go to counseling. She set the appointment, and pleaded with me to go. But, by this time I was really losing it.

I got scared. Suddenly I was scared of everything, frightened every moment. I couldn't follow my thoughts. I couldn't remember when my classes were. One fateful evening I was out on a bike ride and realized it was Wednesday, not Tuesday. I'd missed the one-hour class that would be the sole reason they would take the scholarship away from me. And that really was the beginning of the end.

This feeling, this dark, dark feeling just seeped into every cell in my body and suddenly I was the shell of the person I'd been.

I did try. I kept trying. But in my heart, from that moment on, it was hopeless.

I fought to keep my scholarship. I followed advice to seek help from a counselor, even though I knew she couldn't really help me. I thought she might be able to help me get my scholarship back. She tried. She wrote notes to Miami of Ohio telling them my extreme anxiety had led me to miss that one class. I called the teacher of the class I'd missed and begged her for a chance to make the class up. She said no. It was a one-hour film class. She said no.

I spent all that summer trying to get my scholarship back. I wrote letters. I called. I put all my energy into it. Right before school was going to start in the fall I drove the five hours to Miami of Ohio myself, even though Mom really wanted to come with me. I went before a panel of judges and they said "No. No, no, no no." There is no place for me here in this world.

And for a moment, I thought I just might go back to Miami of Ohio anyway. I mean, what else was I going to do?

But the day before I was to leave, I fell into a pit of regret, of anger, sadness, screaming and pain.

The next morning, Mom found me unresponsive in the neighbor's yard. The doctors in the emergency room could not bring me back. Hours passed. And when I finally opened my eyes I was filled with screaming rage at everything and everyone, especially those who loved me the most.

They transferred me to "Behavioral Health." What the heck, *"behavioral health?* What does that even *mean?*

I was lost.

I was over 18, and the psychiatrist met with me, but I didn't understand a thing she was saying. Something had overtaken my brain. I could barely talk...barely respond.

And I know my parents kept calling, and they were doing everything they could think of to do, but the doctors and therapists wouldn't talk to them because of HIPPA laws, since I was an "adult." Seriously? An adult?

I was, really, "out of my mind." So they put me on some drug, and released me two weeks later, but my time here on earth was already winding down. There was no hope for me. No place for me.

For the next year I went in and out of hospitals. I tried to find some meaning. I tried to hang out with my old friends. But nothing made sense. I didn't know who I was anymore. And now, my ears were paying me back for all the years of loud headphone blasting. They were ringing all the time, and I couldn't hear well at all. I was alone. So alone. And I couldn't let anyone in.

And before I knew it, my anxiety, or whatever you call it, kicked up an unbearable notch. And I knew *'they'* were out to get me. There was nowhere I was safe. They knew where I was, they knew my car, they were in my cell phone, they were everywhere. It was just inevitable. They were going to get me. Everything had a frightening message for me. Every license plate. Every song. It was all around me. THEY were all around me. I was doomed.

The next spring, I was released from another hospital stay because insurance refused to cover the time. And I was scared. Really scared. By now, my doctors were saying I had Schizophrenia, but I knew better. I knew *they* were out to get me. My Mom called the doctor and asked "How can you release him in this state of fear?" And the doctor said "I'm sorry, but your son has a devastating illness."

Sure, they gave me medicines, the doctors did, but they were all in on it. They were all a part of it. Everyone who "loved me" was a part of it. "They were coming to get me and it was going to be bad. The drugs they gave me made me worse. I know they did.

And in September of 2014 I decided I just didn't want to take the prescribed drugs anymore. My Mom, Aunt, Dad and Brother all begged me to stay on them. What did THEY know? They weren't me. They weren't targeted. They weren't going to die anyway, like me.

Then, in November, at my aunt's house, I just couldn't take the fear anymore. I wanted to end it first. In the middle of the night I locked the door, found something sharp, and slit my throat. Even though I was quiet, somehow my aunt and uncle sensed something was wrong, unlocked the door and got me to the hospital for emergency surgery. I emerged with big staples in my neck.

I stayed in intensive care for days. Not speaking. Not really focusing. Stiff and torn. Disappointed. DAMN. I was still here and they were still out to get me. Now what?

Everyone came to tell me they were glad I was alive. I didn't move. Didn't speak. They chanted Nam-myoho-renge-kyo in appreciation for my life, It's the Buddhist chant I'd grown up on, the chant that had made me happy in the past. They sang to me like it was my birthday, they played guitar for me, but what did they know? It was still all over, all over.

I was shipped to Linden Oaks "Behavioral Health." And two weeks later, on a snowy Monday evening, Linden Oaks announced that insurance would no longer pay and said Dad had to come get me. Eyes wide, shoulders hunched, still mostly silent, I walked with him to his car. I looked up, saw the traffic in the street and ran with all my might to get in front of a car to take me out and end my misery. But no. Dad caught me. Boom, I was back in Linden Oaks Hospital. Boom.

Trapped. Bored. Without my music or poetry. I was in purgatory as they looked for someplace to take me, to help me. But there was no place for me in this world. No place. I was on my meds, feeling a little bit better…beating my Mom at chess during visiting hour, and getting used to the routine. Seventy-five days later my counselor found a place in Ohio that would take me.

Mid-February, Mom, Dad and my brother brought me to Hopewell Farm in Ohio.

It was cold. Snowy. Boring. For a few brief moments I had some fun and began remembering who I was. At least I had access to the internet. I ordered some hearing aids. They helped me connect. I could hear what people were saying. Then the fear came back and the highway beckoned with one more escape…

I stepped in front of a quick-thinking semi-truck driver. He avoided hitting me. Just. But what was the use? 'They' were going to get me anyway.

After a stay at a strange hospital in Cleveland – where they could find no place to take me, Mom and Dad brought me to Mom's house but I overdosed the next night and back to Linden Oaks I went. After a while they found me a place called Albany Care in Evanston. And people DID care there. But I was uncomfortable. Scared. Skittish. I began to cheek my meds again and really went out of control.

In a fit of anger, I went to the top of a parking garage in downtown Evanston, and stood on the outside ledge screaming at the top of my lungs. There was an off-duty officer trained in this sort of thing right below me. He and some other fine people saved my life that day.

This time it was different. This time, in Evanston Hospital's emergency room, I came back to life. I just popped out of this trance that had overtaken me. I said "What just happened? What came over me? I'm glad I'm alive." My brother and mom came in and we chanted Nam-myoho-renge-kyo together for as long as the social worker would allow us.

That landed me back in Linden Oaks. But this time...I wanted to live. I wanted to fight. I took all my meds...I went to all their group meetings. I did everything they wanted me to do. I wanted to live for the first time in a long time. I knew 'they' were still out there, but I was chanting with Mom, I was determined. I wanted to live.

And, now that I wanted to live...I was screwed.

Every day, my counselor came to me. "We're looking for a place to take you. No place will take you because of the attempts you've made on your life."

I really wanted to go back to Albany Care. I wanted one more chance, but the director wouldn't give me that chance. My Mom called him just about every day, pleading for one more chance. "No." He said. "I can't risk it. The state will shut me down if Ben comes here and takes his life. And Governor Rauner is already trying to shut us down as it is. We may have to shut our doors by July 1st." Mom told me she was writing letters to officials on Albany Care's behalf, but that didn't change the director's mind. He still said no.

I wanted another chance at life. I took any drug they suggested. Somehow I lost the feeling that my counselor and psychiatrist were out to get me. I was feeling like they were actually on my team.

But, ironically, they still couldn't help me. No place would take me. There was no place to go...no halfway house...no place with professionals to oversee my meds and help me get started on a new road in life. No place where I could make friends and see if I could recover what I'd lost, and make a life for myself. It didn't exist.

There really was no place for me.

Yet, I was happy to be alive. I read every book I could understand. I read voraciously. I could *learn* again. Mom brought me new books and magazines every day, and I read them all. I wanted to understand what was happening in my brain, what had happened to my brain. Why were there so many things I looked back on where I had this eerie feeling that I wasn't there? I wasn't that runner...I wasn't that friend. How could this happen? I studied brain books, and wondered what was really going on. If I wasn't there in my past, who was? I read and read.

My roommate was studying vocabulary words for a test. So I wrote all the words I didn't know, along with their definitions, in the black book Mom got me for writing. Mom and I really enjoyed looking over those words and laughing together. She was an English major and explained how the roots of the words made sense. She brought me big, empty journals and I wrote, I made art, I dreamed. I wrote a page for every year in my life and listed everything I could remember. I quizzed my brain.

Yes, 'they' were still out there, but quieter.

I felt, for the first time, that I could make it. That maybe there could be a place for me. I could smile again. Maybe I could make it. I chanted a lot with Mom. She also did energy healing and EFT (Energy Freedom Technique) Tapping with me.
We only had an hour and a half a day. That's it. Mom would come early and make sure we got the one place that was kind of private in the group dining room. She would give me a back rub, reassure me, tap lightly on the acupressure points on my head. I was getting closer to the Ben I'd been, the Ben I'd lost, and the Ben I still knew.

Mom and I read poetry together every day. I had always loved reading and writing poetry. Now I could *feel* the words like never before.

I was more awake, even though I struggled with the ringing in my ears, and they had taken my hearing aids away, so it was hard to hear.
Mom or Dad or Aunt Alison were there for the short visiting time every day. I really wanted my Linden Oaks counselors to find a place for me to go…where I could live. But nothing was happening. Nothing.

Mom spent every day on the telephone trying to help me. She called the hospital CEO and was referred to someone who listened but took no action. She called everyone she could think of to solve this problem. There had to be somewhere. But no. There wasn't. And insurance was always threatening to stop paying...to just release me to the streets. Mom or Dad would have taken me, but they knew I needed a team of care. I'd proven that during the times they had tried to take me in the past.

And one day I finally got an interview with a place. It sounded great. They promised me the moon and the stars...and called back three hours later, after reviewing my file, to say they couldn't take me...

There was no place for me.

At the end of June, right across from Linden Oaks Behavioral Health, right across the street from the hospital, they put up a summer festival with rides, and live music. I could see it from my window. But I couldn't get to it. I was stuck in the hospital.

This carnival was not for me ~ even though the music stage was yards from my window, yards from my window. I thought of the music, the rides, the families and the fun. None of which I could have. I loved going to carnivals. I loved them. Knowing this was happening, and that I was stuck in here. It was killing me.

The grief of being stuck in this hospital with no place to go just blanketed me. My counselor came to tell me insurance wouldn't pay, and there was no place for me to go. Were they going to release me to the streets? They told only me. I don't think they told my parents that day.

And, the next day…the music started.
I woke up on July 2nd, 2015 to the sound of the music being tested…as I looked out at that stage I couldn't get to, at that carnival for everyone else but me.

My brain was on fire. My brain burned. It was excruciating. After five weeks of being stranded in this hospital, I knew what I had to do.

I wouldn't leave my room. I wouldn't eat. My counselor came to my room, concerned. All I could talk about was the ride called Pharaoh's Fury. I could not get it out of my mind. It was a massive ship that swung up all the way up in the air to one side, came back down through the middle and swung all the way up to the other side…back and forth. It had always been my favorite. Back and forth – up and down. It was all I could think about. All I could talk about.

At noon that day the live music started. The live music I couldn't see…the live music outside my hopeless hospital "no one will take you" prison.

Around 2:00 the counselors let us out in the yard for some fresh air and basketball. I knew what I had to do. I knew what I had to do.

I'm an athlete – small but mighty. I have great strength, even after weeks of shuffling around the hospital in my slippers, I still know what I can do.

I looked at the tall red brick wall separating me and the outside world.

I didn't think.

My body took off in an unbelievable burst of power, anger, decision and might…I sprang right over that wall and landed in the grass, in the outside world…that had no place for me.

I was in a zone. My eyes were fixed. I felt like an animal, moving by instinct, running from habit. I knew how to run.

I ran through the doors of Ribfest carnival. No one stopped me at the gate, even though I paid no entrance fee.

No one talked to me.

No one looked me in the eye.

I went straight to my fate...the ride from my childhood, the humongous swinging boat. Pharaoh's Fury. Straight to it.

"There is no place for me in this world. There is no place for me in this world."

I climbed the back fence of the ride while it was moving....looked up at the huge pendulum of the boat at its highest point and launched my body onto the platform so the boat could swing back down, crushing me in an instant.
Now I could find out if the next world had a place for me...if the next world was the answer...if the next world could finally end my pain, fear, anger, confusion, and knowledge that there truly was no place for me here in this world.

Here one story ends, and other begins. As Ben's mom, and a thirty year practicing Buddhist, (Soka Gakkai, Nichiren, Practical Buddhist, sgi-usa.org), I have always believed that life itself does not die. And I determined to turn poison into medicine and create value for myself and others. Here is my offering.
I knew I could reach my boy, so I began writing him, and our writings continue to this day.

Dear Ben,

Soaring above us all
free and flying
you got your way
you ended your torturous road
you are released
you are released.
And now, you will have all of us
chanting for you
as your mission continues,
right here,
right now, forever.

I will cry until I run out of tears.

I cry in gratitude that you came to me
that we shared these twenty-two years
that we had all those laughs,
and all those tears,
and all those laughs.

My heart will always be full of my Ben,
my Benjamino, my Benjabunny
I am so grateful we took that cruise.
We enjoyed that time.
We explored our world ~

Oh Ben,
Write through me
laugh through me
live your happiness all around me.

My dear boy, I know you never meant to
hurt me. Not ever.

Ben, maybe you're sitting right next to me
on this Friday ~
right here by the pool.
What do you have to say?

Your Loving Mom

Mom,

I did it.

I meant to do it.
~ at the time ~
and I knew it would make you sad,
but somehow I still had to do it.
I had to obey my mind, my legs, my feet,
my incredible surge
of strength and courage.
I could not say no.
It had to happen.
And this story is not yet written,
is not yet told ~
but will be.

My life, and death
HAVE meaning,
Not HAD.

Dearest Mom, my closest friend,
my absolute love, don't despair.
I know you,
       you,
         you
will create a life of meaning,

of love,
of warmth and creativity.

Together we will live on
Together
  we will always live on

Enjoy the sun

  Enjoy this day

    Enjoy your life.

        Your Forever Ben

Dearest boy, how I miss you,
yet I am grateful your suffering is over.
Every day I wake up and wonder if I'm in
some kind of dream.
The thought of never being able to hug you
again, and never hearing your voice just
seems so impossible.
Do you have any words for me,
heart of my heart,
dear child of mine?

Your Loving Mom

Mom,

It is not over. Our love goes on.
Nothing can keep us apart.
Not time.
Not space.
Not death.
Not even death.
We are together forever and ever.
Even if it looks like I am gone
I am not
I am right here beside you
smiling at you
with my arm around you
and running toward you.
Maybe our running towards each other
was the start of my running career
this lifetime.
But you know,
seeing my smile,
feeling our embrace
that this lifetime is not all
is not it...
is not over.

We will live on.
We do live on.

We will always live on.
You. Me.
In every incarnation.
Laughing, loving, with our hearts smiling.
This lifetime, this last one,
I got sick.
I got so sick.
But the next one?
Watch out!
We will be born together
and all that negative karma will be gone
Poof...gone!
And we will share, share, share,
and bask, bask, bask,
bask, bask, bask
in the light of our love.

Your Forever Ben

Ben, Ben, Ben,

Yesterday it was a month.
Today is August 2nd.
And I am filled with appreciation for you,
and for our time together.
I'm sad, sadder than sad can be,
and I'm also filled with hope for the future.
Are you here right now my boy?
Do you have any words for me?

Your Loving Mom

Oh Mom,

I love you so much.
My heart breaks when your heart breaks,
we are one.

Keep spreading the love,

keep being the wonderful person you are
and all you are seeking is coming to you -
go get 'em in that way you have Mom.
Recognize your gifts - be fearless.
What do you have to fear now?
Be bold!

Your Forever Ben

Hi Ben,

I spent yesterday on a boat with some new
friends. I always loved taking you on boats.
You were so alive and happy,
even after you got sick.

Did you join me yesterday?
Are you with me now?
Do you have any words for your sweet
Mommy?

Your Loving Mom

Hi Mom,

Please stop being so sad.
You don't have to prove your love to me by
being sad.
I know you love me.
Please cheer up.
I have.
I'm really happy.
Running with my Aaron, happy with
Michelle, being with you.
I can try harder to be with you,
and it's better if I don't have to try...
if we just have fun together.
Can we do that?

Me: Sure sweetie, is there any way I can make it easier?

Ben:
Be Happy!
Match ME!

Me: Okay Ben,
I'll try to cheer up.

49 days after Ben took flight:

Hi my sweet, sweet boy.
Do you have any words for your Mom?

Hi Mom,
It's great here, no I mean really.
I can do anything I want.
I never have to worry about money,
or my health - or anything.
I'm happy.
Please be happy Mom.
I love you so much Mom,

Your Forever Ben

And later in the car…as I was weeping...
and the song came on, Bridge Over
Troubled Water
by Simon and Garfunkle.

"Sail on Silver girl,
(Silver girl! That's me!)
Sail on by.
Your time has come to shine.
All your dreams are on their way.
See how they shine.
If you need a friend
I'm sailing right behind.
Like a bridge over troubled water
I will ease your mind.
Like a bridge over troubled water
I will ease your mind."

Thanks Ben!

In August I went to Cape Cod
where we had gone almost every year of
Ben's life.

I wrote:

Here,
At the pond -
with one poofy cloud
and no boats,
no people,
and only one bird.
I can imagine the Indians
the quiet
the hush
the respect for the land.
In this quiet -
With no distractions
Do you have any words for me?

Mom,

I couldn't have hoped
for a better Mom than you.
Your patience, your love,
your protection.
You always knew I needed a little more...
A little more love...
A little more touch...
A little more nurturing...
You always knew I could follow my heart.
But you never thought it would lead me to
this.

I will tell you this:
You know the song my soul sings...
and how it loves to laugh.

    Your Forever Ben

And that soul continues to laugh.
I feel him all the time.
Whenever something strikes me funny
I think,
or even say out loud
"Get that Ben?!"
And I know he has shared the joke.

Cape Cod poem to Ben

Here
Where you all played

and ran
and jumped
and yelled.
Here I feel your feet
gently thumping the ground.

Childhood
Motherhood
To do it over again
Be a mother again
have a child
my child
on my lap

His arms around me
wet from the ocean
warm from the fire
Relaxing,
comforting,
Mama-ing,
Oh yes!
Oh Ben,
are you all seeing now?
What do you have for me?

Oh Mom,

Be free, be happy, be warm.
Live where you want to live.
Find your perfect spot.

> *Do what you want to do.*
> *Be who you want to be.*

Mom, be you.
Warm, happy, lovable you.

Your Forever Ben

Because, my son

Starting
a whole new life -

I would have preferred a life with *you*
my boy ~
Boy who lit up the room with his smile
Boy with
   perfect
       comic
          timing
Boy who made my heart sing.

But that's not what I got.
No, instead, I am in the third month of my
life without you.
Readying myself to fly.
I've lived in the cold my whole life.
Florida here I come!

Monday morning,
~ filled with the rhythm of chanting
Nam myoho renge kyo...

Ben?

Mom,

I'm your angel -
always here
Your eternal cheerleader
Your great love
your fun light.
You will find your ONE.
I will help.
Stay strong
Stay guided
Stay you

Your Forever Ben

October, 2015

Hi my sweet, sweet boy.

Did you hear?
I'm going to go to
John Denver week in Aspen!
Isn't that great?

I am in the sun,
in one of my favorite places,
thinking of my sweet, sweet boy.

Do you have anything to say to me?

Your Loving Mom

Oh come on Mom,
You know I wasn't always sweet.
(Big smile!)
I could be a real jerk too!
I'm glad you're outside.
I'm glad you'll be having
a fall to remember.
I am glad you're living your life.
Try not to feel sad. Okay?
Try to be happy.
You have so much to look forward to
If only you could see what I see.
If only you could see what I see.
I love you Mom,

Your Ben

Later I wrote:

My dear boy.
I don't care what you say
about not being sweet.
As far as I'm concerned,
sweetness was your essence -
through and through -
my wonderful boy.
Do you have any words for me,
my boy…
boy who came to earth through my body…
boy I wanted to grow old with by my side
in the flesh…

What say you?

Mom,

I am here with my arm around you always.
Keep walking.
Keep drinking water.
Keep feeling better and you will feel better.
I will help.
Your Ben

And I wrote:

Loving Mother's lament

The child
Your love, our love, is born.
And all attention - all thought -
all love immediately has a focus.
All the stored love
Just waiting
pours out
and from that moment
flows toward that little face,
that little body,
that smile,
that giggle,
those eyes,

And it magnifies over and over
throughout the years.

As that child, that very child
delights you over and over
and the love grows and grows…

And then suddenly -
suddenly ~
Where do we put our love now?
Where does that excess -
no, not excess before,
but excess NOW,
Where does that love go?
Is it in my pocket?
Can I turn it on myself?
Please?

Oh Mom,

I love you so much.
I'm so proud of you.
and excited for you.
You have a great future.
You will have love.
*You **are** love.*
*You **are** love.*
Please remember.
Remember all the best times.
Remember the running.
And the sunsets,
with our arms around each other.
Remember running to each other
in the glow of our extraordinary love.
Oh Mom,
I know sometimes it doesn't help to say
we are always together
when you can't hold me
or see my children.
I know how much
you longed to see my children
and be their grandmother
and I'm really sorry that won't happen.
Really so sorry.
I'm looking for a man for you.

A man with grandchildren and a family
with warm hearts
to enfold you
In the meantime ~
Keep it up Mom,
I'm so proud of you.

Your Forever Ben

My Ben,

Right There

It's always right there
behind my eyelids
In my very next breath
at the crest of the next thought

YOU, my son, my boy, my baby
my baby boy.

Oh yes,
I know it was unbearable
I know you were stuck
I know you burned

And now,
and for the rest of my life,
with every thought
with every breath
It is my challenge to live without you
Without your smile
Your sparkling eyes
Your quick wit and our shared unique
laughter
My darling darling son.
 Ben

When I can change
that everyday punch in the gut

To appreciation
To brightness

To knowledge that your bright flame
Burns on
    For me
        For you
            For the world
And when I can conjure our happiest
moments
And hold them

treasured in joy
Rather than burning and pain

I will have done some magic indeed.

My dear boy
Have you been reborn again?
Are you in someone's belly?
Are you still here nonetheless?
Do you have any words for me?

Mom,

I always have words for you
And I will always have words for you.
Forever. Always.
I will be here when you write to me,
think of me, long for me.
I'm always here,
a beautiful part of me is always with you.
Always cares
always close…
I feel so much wiser now.
I'm not on meds
I'm not sick
My being is clear,
my soul is released.
And I am here for you
Not in the same way.
Not in the same way.
I'm constantly loving you,
Sending you love
Sending you ideas,
Sending you sunshine.
Mom, maybe you should go get that coloring
book and color.

Your Forever Ben

Benjamino

Whom I miss with all my heart
With all my heart
I'm so pissed I have to live
the rest of my life without you
I'm really, really pissed
I just don't see the point
I mean really, why did I choose this life
If it had to be filled with so much pain?
Here I am searing in pain missing you
Simmering in anger and angst
And lonelier than lonely can be.
Darling Ben
What do you have to say to me?

Hi Mom,

I'm here. I'm with you.
Have faith.
Don't give up.
You are also on your way to all you want.
I know it's hard
I know it's hard
But Sometime down the road
And I don't know when,
You will look back on 2015 and think:
"That is the year
that changed my life for the better."
Even though you don't know it
or feel it at the time
I'm here with you Mom.
Part of me never leaves you.
Not even for a minute.
I'm right here,
right here with your beautiful angels
They feel so blessed to be with you!

Your Forever Ben

A few days later
there was a beautiful sunset.
I watched it - with Ben beside me.

And when I came back inside I asked him:
Ben ~ do you have any words for me?

Mom,

It was great
watching that sunset with you.
I'm always with you, you know.
I remember that time
we were in Whitlock Park
watching the sunset together
And it seemed like
the sky and the ground had reversed.
I remember you running in saying
"Ben come with me to see the sunset!"
And how we sat and watched it together
and all those sunsets on the cruise.
I loved that time with you Mom.
Tonight was great.
Thanks for sharing it with me
I love you so much Mom.

Your Forever Ben

The first Christmas without him ~

Dear Ben, Benjamin, Benjabunny,
Ben Ben, My son.

It's December twenty-third.
Before we know it Christmas will be here.
Let's remember all the great moments,
All the fun memories.
All the excitement with Grandma,
Aunt Boo…
You and your brother Aaron
helping me with the soup.
You were always my little buddies.
What a lucky Mom I was!

My sweet sweet boy.
Even when you pulled away I still knew
we were bonded for life,
and forever… not just life…
And, my sweet boy, do you have some
words for me?

            Your loving Mom

Awww Mom,

Please do your best
to keep a light heart this Christmas.
Remember all the fun, fun times.
Think of all the laughs
Remember all the years before I got sick ~
because they were great.
You gave me a great life, Mom.
You and Dad, you were the best.
You always believed in me
more than I believed in myself.
You brought me up on the beach,
in the sun,
on the sand,
in your arms.

Your Forever Ben

In deepest darkest January I wrote:

Dear Ben,
Dear Angels,
Dear any loving one who wants to help,
what words do you have
for this hopeless soul in sun-less Chicago
at a time I feel so blue?

           This loving soul

Hi Mom,

I know.
I know you feel sad.
I feel sad with you.
I recognize the feeling.
It sucks.
All I can say is
I know you feel no hope,
But I feel enough hope for both of us.
I think you should further explore EFT
tapping.
It was really helping you.
Keep chanting
Go Mom go!
Get out of the cold!

I am here loving you all the time.

Your Forever Ben

In February I awakened into a dream of Ben
hugging me.

I wrote to him:

Oh my darling boy,
thank you for coming
and giving me a happy hug.
Is there anything you'd like to say to me
now?

Hi Mom, (in a peppy voice)
.
I wish you could stop thinking
there was something you could've done.
There was nothing you could have done.

I just had to know
what was on the other side.
I just had to know.
And I'm happy.
Please be happy too!

Your Forever Ben

I regretted not buying Ben a dog
when he was a child.
In his journals he wrote
if he had a dog
he would name him Snickers
And the other day in my living room
someone talked about
a dog named Snickers.
I just had to laugh
"Ben, did you hear that?"
And I wrote:

Ben!

Are you enjoying all the doggies on other
side?
Do you have any words for me?

Oh Mom, yes, yes!
There are dogs galore!
So much love and cuddles.
And I can be any age with them!

You're tired. Have sweet dreams Mom

Your forever and ever Ben

January 24th, Sunday

Hi Ben bud, my baby boy.

I know you are not my baby.
And in fact…
you are not mine.
You are the world's Ben Silver.
Benjamin Lee Silver.

I love you with all my heart.
I'm thinking of you.
And I'm ever grateful you came to me…
my boy, our boy, the world's boy.

Your loving Mom

Oh Mom,

I love you so much,
you know how I love you.
Right now
I'm wrapping my arms around you
and singing to you
and holding you close.
It's me who loves you,
within words,
beyond words,
beyond the power of expression,
beyond all thought,
Here I am,
here you are,
together in our eternal dance.
Mom, the road is open for you, for me.
Let's dance together forever.
Be happy Mom.
Be healthy.
Be the joyous spreading
of happiness you are.
I love you so much Mom.
I always have.
I always will.
                    Your Forever Ben

p.s. I can be whatever height I want.
I can be anything and anywhere.
I can fly!

Hi My sweet boy,

I feel so close to you right now.
I'm thinking of you now ~ not then.
Now - in all your glory,
in your magnificent, expanded state,
all potentiality,
all YOU ~ self-expressed, beautiful ~
All YOU
and wondering what words you have
for this being I am right now,
sitting here, writing you.

Your Loving Mom

Mom, yes.
   Mom, yes.

All expansive, all seeing me.
It is everything I hoped for
How can I describe a state free from
frustration?
No money to be made,
nothing to prove,
no one to compare myself to,
aware of all my goodness,
all everyone's goodness,
all the colors,
all the breadth of life.
How can this be so
when the word
most commonly used for this state
is "death?"
When it isn't that at all.
I can tell you this ~
I don't know the answer
to all those questions.
I just have the experience of it.
That's it.
And I feel consumed - no - the opposite -
radiating the essence of love.
And you can feel it and bask in it.

I am sending the rays your way -
everyone's way!
This is so neat.

But I don't want you,
or anyone else,
to think this is so much better
that they (or you)
should just come join me here.

No. You stay.
You bask in the physical right now.
You and that love of yours are so close
Mom.
Do not give up hope.
Do not give up hope for your body.
Do not give up hope for your health,
for your fitness, for your energy,
for your sparkling career.
No Mom. You've got it ALL
and you've got me ALL the time –
while awake -
while sleeping.
*I am always ~ and always **will** be ~*
with you,
I bask and reflect in your love.
I loved being your son,

and you are the rockingest Mom ever.

And I love you now…
your openness, your light,
your warmth, your spark,
only now, now, I can be loving you,
and not in that excruciating pain I was in.
So much better.
Mom, rest your eyes.
Rest your heart.
Breathe.
Sleep.
I love YOU,

> *Your Forever Ben ~*
> *Forever and ever!*

Later, as the pain comes and goes,
and comes back…
I write:

Ben, Ben, Ben, Ben
my darling boy.
Do you have any words for your Mom,
who is really in so many kinds of pain?
Every day I wake up and give it my all. I
give my speeches, I chant for you, for all my
friends, and for all the world. And there's a
hole in my life…missing you.

Your Loving Mom

Hey Mom,

I really wish you could hear my voice.

Can you hear it ~
in your head?

I just love you.
Maybe you can watch
"Sailing with my Mama"
(Ben's original song to me)

Because that's what I'd do
 if I were with you,
and if I were well,
I would sing to you.
Don't give up hope.
Treat yourself well.
Feel good Mom.
Bring the sunshine from within.
You can do this.
You've done it before,
You can do it again.

And buy those tickets for Florida.
Have something to look forward to...
I'm here!

I'm here!
I'm always here!
I'm watching.
I'm holding your hand.
I'm holding your hand.

Your loving son,
loving you,

Your Forever Ben

April 17, 2016

Hi Ben, we've made progress on Ben's Memorial Mile. We are holding an event to bring the running community together to run, cheer, remember you and raise money for schizophrenia research.

It will honor you, and make a difference.

What words do you have to say to your sweet Mom?

Oh Mom,

I get it.
I see how hard it is for you.
I get it.
But look at you,
putting one foot in front of the other,
and you even bought a car –
the car you wanted.
Well done.
It's a cushy car, that's for sure!
I'm proud of you.
Great job!
I'm here, I'm here.
All the time.
Forever and ever.
Let your heart lighten Mom.
I'm sending my smile into your heart.
Be light.
Be happy.
Enjoy this day.
Enjoy this sunny day.

Your Forever Ben

Ben's Aunt Alison (my sister) and I were on the cover of the Downers Grove Reporter promoting Ben's Memorial Mile.

I wrote to Ben:

So much is being done in your name, Ben.
I'm wondering if you knew.
Could you possibly have known
you'd be leaving so soon?
I saw a picture of me and you -
you were my baby on my lap
with your head on my shoulder
and I thought
"Maybe that's why Ben
always stayed so close…"

What say you my boy?

Hi Mom,

Maybe, maybe part of me did know
that my life would be short.
Maybe part of me did,
and that's the reason
I gave myself to love you so fully,
and never held back.
Maybe....

Your Forever Ben

The other day I met a dog called "Benjie"
and I just laughed.
I wrote to Ben:

A dog?
Ben?
Benjie?
Very funny. Very funny!
What amazing anything do you have for me
now?

Hi Mom,

Hah!
Yes, I know.
Sometimes it feels unreal.
I know
sometimes it feels unreal to me.
I look at you looking at my pictures
and I think

"Boy, did that lifetime even happen?"
It went by in a flash –
in the wink of an eye."

I know you and I were focusing on all the
good times…
All the things that went incredibly right.
All the thrills,
because it was a thrilling life
wasn't it Mom?
From the first moments in San Francisco -
all the friends, beaches, laughter, play
~ remember the monkey game?
Me in the trees?
I was a monkey.
I was a monkey
I know for at least a few lifetimes!

Ben - the monkey -
and so much more.
At the beach with Aaron.
Hawaii.
John Denver.
Joan. Danielle, John, Dimitri.
Donna. Peppino. Aleza.
Artwork.
The San Francisco School -
where we were treated with respect.
Highland. The rough ride,
then Mrs. Brown. My poetry,
Being cast as Bilbo
and running, running, running.
Dances, Sara and prom.
So happy to be a part of all of it.
It could be easy to forget about college.
I guess I did make a few friends
before I got entirely lost.
But Mom, it's all good.
Especially now.
You don't have to try so hard anymore…
or worry so much.
I know you never meant to let me go.
You never, ever wanted to let me go,
and you know you don't have to.
I'm right here.

I'm gonna really enjoy
Ben's Memorial Mile
and I hope you do too.
It's going to be something like nothing else.
A celebration
(like that Mom? Celebration is playing on
your iPod right now)
Don't I have the most perfect timing?
I'm more powerful than I've ever been -
and happy Mom,
except when I see you suffering.
Don't. Mom.
Keep tapping, keep walking, keep chanting.
Keep being your own unique combination
of sweet, smart, creative
Just be yourself Mom -
Content in every moment,
like you teach so many others.
Enjoy your own teachings Mom.
And most of all,
love yourself.
Love your loving, loving self.
I love you.
I always, always will.

Your Forever and ever Ben.

Mother's Day 2016

I wrote to Ben:

"A whole new world
with new horizons to perceive
Let me share
this whole new world with you."
(from Aladdin)

I'll bring you everywhere with me my
Forever Ben.

Oh Ben - you were too beautiful for this
world.
Too beautiful and loving and kind.
Too beautiful.

Awe Mom,

Thank you –

I came from you.

I came
　　from
　　　　you

Not just biologically
my spirit,
my Ben-ness came from you.
My spirit to make everyone smile,
my light,
my darkness,
my humor,
my irony,
my poetry,
my light,
my heart,
my love for lovely, lovely you.
Please love yourself Mom.
Please banish your fear -
Please go live your dreams - be happy, be
healthy.
Take great care of yourself

and laugh more than ever.
You, Mom,
and your warm heart and spirit ~
you are light itself.

Meditate, tap, chant,
have fun with everyone.
Keep your wits about you
and for goodness sake
don't beat yourself up all the time.
It
   does
      no
        good
Want good?
Search for praise.
Remember the good times
with a song in your heart.
You've said many times how lucky you are
to have had all those years
 together with me.
Let's savor their memory.
Let's bask in the glow of them.
Starting right now - Right Now.

        Your Forever Ben

In the plane heading to California to celebrate Aaron Michael Silver's joyous graduation from Loyola Medical School (Ben's older brother),
I sat next to an Olympic figure skater's mother. She was telling me about the life of a champion skater, and as I listened to her my tears began flowing down my cheeks remembering my boy, my champion. My runner.

I picked up my pen and paper and Ben wrote:

Awe Mom,

It's okay.
I did my life.
I'm happy with my life.
I did what I wanted this lifetime.
It was perfectly perfect –
Even though it might be hard for you,
or others to see it that way.
Look at all the things I did.
I skied.
I danced.
I ran.
I laughed.
I chanted.
I had friends.
I had a girlfriend.
I lived a really full life in my 22 years.
And I have no regrets.
Well, I do have a few regrets,
And that's when I see you or Dad, Aunt
Alison, Aaron
Or anyone else sad.
I know.
I miss you too.

But please remember my brain was sick.
Please remember my brain was sick.
It's just the way it was.
And we couldn't do anything about it.
It was just that way.

But Ben's Memorial Mile...
That's really something Mom –
Maybe they will figure out
what went wrong in my brain.
Maybe they will figure out
how to fix people's brains
So they are not in pain
and not causing pain for others.
There has to be hope.
There has to be hope.

We started this thing and it will live on.
And I've said it before,
But let me say it again:
Mom, I'm right here.
I'm right here in your heart.
I'm right here in your arms.
I'm here gazing into your eyes.
I'm here laughing with you
When you see something funny.
I came to see you off this morning

As a big grey heron taking flight.
It's all real.
It's all real.

So, I know it's hard.
I know it seems like we're separated.
But you see me everywhere – you really do.
Even on memories on Facebook, right?

And I do have a message
for Ben's Memorial Mile
and it's this:

All you have to do is pick up a pen.
Death isn't "death."
It's not here on earth in the same way;
It's just a different vibration.
But it's awareness.
It's something.
Not nothing.
And there is no judgement –
Not from me –
Not towards me.
It's just that "poof"
This life was over right here.

I'm rambling.

And I know you're wondering
What anyone will say about this,
And how they will take it.
But it's true.
Close your eyes.
I'll still be right here.

Your Forever Ben

That last letter was written just before Ben's Memorial Mile for the edition I printed in honor of the event. Over 400
people gathered at Downers Grove North High School's outdoor track on June 11th, 2016. There were mile races for fast runners, a mile for walkers, a few shorter races for kids and my favorite, "Ben's Costume Mile." At the end of the costume mile, the three costumed Ninja Turtles waited at the finish line for each other so they could cross the line together. It was a beautiful event...with a gorgeous sunset that lit up the sky and lasted forever. I could feel Ben every moment. Hope for the Day was there, along with NAMI DuPage and One in Four,

and Your Story Counseling. Some other excellent organizations are the Brain and Behavior Institute which funds Schizophrenia research. Alliance of Hope for Suicide Loss Survivors hosts forums online to help anyone. Catholic Charities LOSS group helped me personally through free and excellent counseling.

I am grateful to all individuals and organizations who are working to better the world of Mental Health.

Right after Ben's Memorial Mile I fulfilled my dream of moving to Florida. And I managed to do it with the help of some very devoted friends. I was in Florida by the time the year anniversary of Ben's death came along. On that day, July 2nd I was planning to spend most of the day chanting. Then it turned out my friend who had driven with me was available to play.

I wrote to Ben:

Hi Ben,

I'm sitting here looking at the vast, blue, changing, yet unchanging ocean, wondering how you feel my sweet, sweet boy.

Wow Mom.

Gorgeous. Another sunny, spectacular day.
I know you're going to love it here in
Florida - and if, by some chance you don't ~
you will find your space.
I know you will.
A year.
A year.
The first thing I want to say is
I love how you are not dwelling in the past.
Yes, you're "honoring" my memory and
you're chanting.
And really Mom,
Today is just like any day.
I don't say that to get you mad,
or more upset.
Today may be July 2nd,
but don't forget I am eternal.
I am your eternal ben.
Calendar days only matter to me
because they matter to you
Personally I'd much rather
you do something fun for you, or even, yes,
Buy something memorable
or talk to someone memorable
than spend the whole day praying.

Now, I know you like to chant,
but look at you Mom
Look at what you set into motion.
Look right now at the waves on the beach
Lit up by the sun.
That's me.
That's you.
We're coming in
All bright and happy and bouncy
And landing in the right place.
Look at you coming into your own place.
Your coming into your own job, own man,
Own good fortune by the writing of your
(and my) book.
All is possible Mom.
All is possible.
You've already proven it.
There's no need to cry and fret
And live over that day,
Unless you want to.
It's a beautiful Saturday in sunny Florida.
What a day for making memories.

And what I meant about the waves,
In case you think I was being obtuse
Is, it's happening,
It will happen

The trajectory is set
And it's great -
Full on - determined
In your everyday prayers.

You got this Mom
      You got this.

Your Forever Ben
Go get yourself a flower lei!

~~~~~~

Ben's story is not over. It is my deep desire that my sharing of Ben's story will be a catalyst for changing the world of mental health. I see a need for holistic treatments and drugs that do not have side effects that cause someone to go off them, thus triggering psychotic episodes. I see a need for treatment centers that can help people get a new start in life, and where music and the arts are celebrated. I see a need for hope. Hope for our loved ones who are struggling. Hope for those who have lost loved ones to suicide. If you are suffering, please reach out. As Hope For The Day says "It's OK not to be OK." Reach out.

Acknowledgements
Ben, thank you for choosing me as your Mom this lifetime.
It was a mystical, beautiful, exciting ride, and it still is.
Every day I love you. Every day I think of you.

Thank you to my Daddy and Stepmom, Barry and Janis Newbery. You have been with us every step of the way. Ben adored you.

Thanks my sweet Mommy. You made me the colorful girl I am. I know you and Ben are up there talking politics!

Thank you "Aunt Boo" for giving us all the gift of music.

Thank you Aaron Michael Silver M.D., Ben chose YOU as his loving brother. You make me proud every day. You were the best brother Ben could have ever had, and my thoughtful, loving, inspiring son!

Thank you Alison and Frank Danta, Ben's aunt and uncle. You saved him, over and over with your love. Thank you.

Thank You Tyler Harpster, your cousin Ben adored you.

Thank you Paul Silver, my "wusband" and the father of our boys. You gave it your all. You always did, and always will.

Thank you Meg, Darryl and Lisa Groom. You've been a great support for Aaron and us all! Your beauty, your hearts and your wonderful wines enrich us all!

Thank you Dr. Josh Silver. You are a brilliant doctor and wonderful nephew. Thanks for moving to St. Petersburg Florida and welcoming me here. Thanks Nikki Lee Ezelle, your beautiful intelligence and smart techie skills make this an easier world! I know you would have loved Ben.

Thank you entire Silver family! Susan and Joel, Rachel, Anne and Matthew, Gary and Meredith, Adam, Haley, Justin and Garrett, Allan and Jen, Daniel and Eric, and Uncle Richard Warwick. Aunt Arie and "Uncky" Frost. .

Thank you Jackie Silver, Aaron and Ben's grandmother. Your generosity has deeply touched the lives of all your children and grandchildren. Thanks Eddie Lee Dobbins, my oldest friend, your book, "Tea With Mom" will shine.

Thanks Katie Kenck Seidenschwarz, my second oldest friend, for our John Denver friendship. Mary Lostarakos, dear, dear friend, full of laughter and warmth, I love you so much! Kindred Willow Kai, your massages are heavenly, I love your beautiful bright light of beauty, come back to sunny Florida!! Joy Lucinda, your energy and essential oil healings got me though the hardest times and your inspiring journey lights my way, Michelle and Gary Wealther, those days on your boat healed my soul. Thanks for your help with my move. I can't wait until you move to Florida! Thank you Matayman for the gift you are. Thank you Tracy DeHart, I never could have moved to Florida without your help! Kate Randolph, my dear friend and Buddhist mentor, you are my treasure. Hal and Sarah Randolph, Ben loved you so, Amy, Ian and Andrew Flynn in San Anselmo, Ca, thanks for our long friendship, the "Flynn Inn," and for coming to Chicago to be with me in my darkest days, Thank you Joan Strasser for your years of friendship, hiking, political insight and for giving us *Hop on Pop* so Aaron could learn to read. I wish Ben could have found his own Shrader House. Danielle (soul mother of my boys), John, Dimitri and Atreus Canaris, thank you for being part of my family. Etjen Palmer, the love-goddess of the universe. I can't wait until you write your book! Donna Wapner, Peppino and Aleza D'Agostino you make the world a more beautiful and melodious place. Thanks Kathy Fisher, our daily conversations got me through. Thanks for being my friend in faith. Melissa Bradford, you are setting the world of education on fire, thank you for founding the Sudbury school, and giving Ben a great place to volunteer, and thank you for introducing me to "unschooling." Deborah House, thank you for coming to chant every morning. You got me through the hardest times. Amos Snell, you walked with Martin Luther King, and you walked with me when I was a Baby Buddhist, thanks for all your wise guidance. Gene O'Connell, my inspiring Buddhist mentor. Thank you for being with me in the delivery room with both my boys! Your heart as a nurse and hospital CEO shines! Betsy Grimm, my EFT Tapping friend, thanks for grounding me here in Florida. Georgine

Bellandi, thank you for coming to chant with me every morning for a year, you are a treasure. Thank you Nina Dixon Scheinkman. You inspire me. Let's win together! Diana Sakolari, Angela Gambino, thanks for your friendship and all our good times. Ginny Zemel, you stepped in to create the most inspiring Life Celebration for Ben, my gratitude is boundless for your loving spirit, I love you. Jenny-Fox Anderson, my college roommate, thanks for all the notes and love, I knew you were with me. Thanks to our family friends, Larry and Bebe, Michael and Michelle Lifson, the world is a better place because of the light you shine so brightly. My sons were lucky to have you as best friends, and our days watching our boys run will live forever in our lives. Thank you Bill and Connie, Jacob and Sam Brower. Without you, Ben's Memorial Mile would not have happened. Thank you for all your hard work and for giving our committee a home. Thanks John Walter Smiles and Jared Wissmuller, our running family and devoted Ben's Memorial Mile members. Thanks Annette Bonfield and all the families from Downers Grove North and the surrounding schools who came out for Ben's Life Celebration and Memorial Mile. Thank you Coach Kupich, John Sipple and Glenn Bicichi. You are family. Thank you to Downers Grove North and all the runners who touched our lives. Thank you Amy McNicholas. Thank you for being the best therapist I've ever had, at a time I needed it most. Thank you to my mentor Daisaku Ikeda and the Soka Gakkai International. Thank you to all the readers of chantforhappiness.com. Thanks Mark Lutnes, Morag Waghorn, Neha Sharma and Karla. Throughout Ben's illness I could feel your chanting, and look, we are turning poison into medicine.

Thanks to all at Cantata Adult Life Services.

Thanks Dan Urben for coming to Ben's life celebration and understanding. My heart is full of gratitude to you for your warm support during the year after Ben died. Thanks

Nancy Vlasak for your warm sense of humor and smarts, and for your support at all my speaking events. Thanks Jesus, Lisa Capone, Lisa Hobin, Mary Allen, Marie Bolson, Brenda Johnson, and Jennifer Tan. Thanks for being such a great place to work during Ben's illness, and throughout my first year after he died. I will always be grateful for you.

And thank you to all my new friends in Florida, especially Gig Guthrie who found me a wonderful place to live, And Gina and Johnnie Machado for renting me this gorgeous haven overlooking the gulf. Thanks Mary Shehade and Ed Talbot, the most active and fun couple ever! Thanks Michaela Holmes, and Eileen Oertel, and Julliann Collins for being my new girlfriends in Florida. Thank you Ric Krajewski for rescuing me in so many different ways. Thanks Fran McCarthy, Nina Bauer, Kristy Cordellio , Corinne Ericsson, Rafil Q Hughes for being my new friends in faith here.

Thank you Dave Kunicki and Ben Mattson, for your partnership and Jonathan S. Boucher, founder of Hope For The Day. Your vision made this book come alive. Your insights, your hearts, your HOPE help so many. May your great work continue to spread!

Dear Reader,

I write to you with sorrow for the loss of so many world-wide to suicide. But I also have hope. I have hope because I *know* that expressing ourselves, and sharing the stories of our loved ones, can be a blessing to both ourselves and others in truly a myriad of predictable and also quite unforeseen ways. From writing therapy to contemporary mindfulness and acceptance based cognitive therapy, a stream of avenues of evidence converge on the incredible power of self-expression.

The organization for which I serve as Executive Director, Hope for the Day, focuses on just this. Spearheaded by our anchor initiative, *It Only Takes One,* we awaken each morning in order to break the silence and shatter the aura of stigma around discussing mental health and suicide. Both our lived experiences, and the empirical data, have demonstrated that simply *starting the conversation* can be like lifting an enormous weight off of your back. Just by initiating honest conversations with our loved ones and throughout our community we can literally save lives.

I would like to express my gratitude to, and admiration for Jamie in sharing the story of her son, Ben Silver. While Ben's story is unique, at the same time his struggle with our current mental health care system is anything but uncommon. We desperately need more Jamie Lee Silvers in this world--for those who have been touched by suicide to come forth and talk about it, so that others can heal. Sometimes, *It Only Takes One* story of struggle, expressed with passion and hope, to unlock the voices of others just waiting to break free.

Most Sincerely,

Dave Kunicki,MBA
Executive Director, Hope for the Day

For more information about It Only Takes One, please visit: *www.ItOnlyTakesOne.org*

Quotes by Daisaku Ikeda, the President of the Soka Gakkai International. All quotes are from **Ikedaquotes.org**

Hope transforms pessimism into optimism. Hope is invincible. Hope changes everything. It changes winter into summer, darkness into dawn, descent into ascent, barrenness into creativity, agony into joy. Hope is the sun. It is light. It is passion. It is the fundamental force for life's blossoming.

Activity is another name for happiness. Give free, unfettered play to your unique talents, live with the full radiance of your being. This is what it means to be truly alive.

No matter how hopeless or bleak things appear, the moment always comes when suddenly our spirit revives, and hope is reborn. That is why we must never give up.

When we possess the treasure of hope, it gives rise to other treasures, too. Hope draws forth our inner potential and strength. Hope is a magic weapon that enables us to make our dreams come true.

No matter how long the cold, bleak days of winter may continue, winter always turns to spring. This is the law of the universe and the law of life. As long as we hold on to hope, spring is sure to come.

"Hope," Beethoven cried, "you forge the heart into steel." Hope is confidence. Hope is determination. Hope is courage. And faith is the ultimate expression of hope. Belief fortifies the heart.

As long as one has hope, there is nothing one cannot achieve; everything is born from hope.

Human beings are inherently endowed with the power to bring out the best possible results from the worst possible circumstances.

It is vital to have a resilient spirit so that without complaints or feelings of disaffection, one is able to always look on the bright side of a situation and find in it a source of hope and happiness. Such wisdom makes it possible to lead a thoroughly fulfilled life.

Though it might be difficult to appreciate at first, the "mud" of our suffering provides the building material from which we can erect a solid bulwark for the palace of happiness within. The deeper the mire of suffering, the more indomitable a palace we can establish.

Buddhism teaches that whatever our individual circumstances, we can always discover the capacity to help others; it also assures us that those who have suffered the most have the right to the greatest happiness.

The experience of losing a loved one impels us toward a deeper understanding of life. Everyone fears and is saddened by death. That is natural. But by struggling to overcome the pain and sadness that accompanies death, we become sharply aware of the dignity and preciousness of life and develop the compassion to share the sufferings of others as our own.

Resolve to be the "sun." Then no matter what problems you may face, the dawn will always break, fine weather will always return, and spring will never fail to come.